Anonymous

The Greeting of the Ward of Castle Baynard to its Alderman

The Rt. Hon. David Evans, F.R.G.S., Lord Mayor of London, 9th November, 1891

Anonymous

The Greeting of the Ward of Castle Baynard to its Alderman
The Rt. Hon. David Evans, F.R.G.S., Lord Mayor of London, 9th November, 1891

ISBN/EAN: 9783744736220

Printed in Europe, USA, Canada, Australia, Japan

Cover: Foto ©ninafisch / pixelio.de

More available books at **www.hansebooks.com**

Right Honourable DAVID EVANS, F.R.G.S.,
LORD MAYOR OF LONDON,
1891-92.
Alderman of the Ward of Castle Baynard.

(From a Negative by The London Stereoscopic Company, Limited.)

THE GREETING

OF

The Ward of Castle Baynard

to its ALDERMAN,

THE RT. HON. DAVID EVANS, F.R.G.S.,

LORD MAYOR OF LONDON,

9th November, 1891.

"*The City of London is the cradle of all our great establishments, and of the civil and religious liberties of the land.*"—HENRY BROUGHAM.

Privately Printed for the Reception Committee of Castle Baynard Ward.

BLADES, EAST & BLADES,
Printers,
23, ARCHURCH LANE, LONDON, E.C.

CONTENTS.

	PAGE
Frontispiece. Plate used by the Ward	4
Members of the Court of Common Council for the Ward	5
The Address to the Lord Mayor	6
The Lord Mayor's Reply ...	7
A Record, &c. (Title page)	8
An Antiquarian Ramble through the Ward ...	9
Some Aldermen of the Ward who have served as Lord Mayor ...	19
Note as to same	22
Lord Mayors having a Welsh lineage	25
Alderman Wilson's Bequest	27
Assistance of Dean and Chapter, and of the Richmond Herald ...	29
Model Baynard Castle (illustrated) ...	30
Shields placed on the Model (illustrated) ...	32
Ludgate Hill decorated (illustrated) ...	34
St. Paul's Church Yard (illustrated)	35
Extract from *The Times* ...	36
,, *The Evening Standard*	37
Proceedings of preliminary Meeting of the Members of the Ward	39
Notice convening a Public Meeting of the Inhabitants of the Ward	40
Proceedings at the Public Meeting	41
The Reception Committee ...	42
Proceedings of the Reception Committee ...	43
Deputation to attend on reading the Address	46
Proceedings of the Decoration Sub-Committee	47
,, ,, Address Sub-Committee	48
,, ,, Collectors	50
Notice convening the Wardmote on 21st December, 1891	51
Proceedings at the Wardmote	52
List of Subscribers to the Decorations	53

The Frontispiece Plate

Used on the Official Notices issued by the Ward Clerk of Castle Baynard.

Castle Baynard Ward

Members of the Court of Common Council for The Ward of Castle Baynard.

Alderman.

THE RIGHT HON. DAVID EVANS, F.R.G.S., LORD MAYOR.
Elected Common Councilman, 1874.
,, Alderman, 1884.
,, Sheriff of London and Middlesex, 1885.
,, Lord Mayor, 1891.

Commoners.

WILLIAM THORNBURGH BROWN, ESQ., DEPUTY. Elected 1875.
Chairman Cattle Markets Sub-Committee, 1883.
,, Finance and Parliamentary Sub-Committee, 1885.
,, City of London School Committee, 1886.
,, Orphan School Committee, 1889.
Appointed Deputy of the Ward, 1889.
Chairman Lord Mayor and Sheriffs' Committee, 1891.

EDGAR FRANCIS JENKINS, ESQ. Elected 1880.
Chairman Officers and Clerks Committee, 1884.
,, General Purposes Committee, 1887.
,, Library Committee, 1889.

GEORGE THISTLE THORNES, ESQ. Elected 1885.
Chairman Port of London Sanitary Committee, 1890.
,, Sanitary Committee of the Sewers, 1891.

ARTHUR BYRNE HUDSON, ESQ., F.S.I. Elected 1885.

JOHN CHARLES CHUBB, ESQ. Elected 1886.

WILLIAM PORTER, ESQ. Elected 1890.

CHARLES VALENTINE HUNTER, ESQ. Elected 1890.

ALEXANDER RITCHIE, ESQ. Elected 1890.

Ward Clerk.

F. W. LEWIS FARRAR, ESQ. Elected 1866.

The Address

Read at the gateway of the Model Baynard Castle, in St. Paul's Church Yard, by W. Curling Anderson, Esq., on behalf of the inhabitants of the Ward, to the Right Hon. David Evans, Lord Mayor, Alderman of the Ward of Castle Baynard, in his State Coach, drawn by six horses, and attended by his Chaplain, Sword Bearer, and Mace Bearer, on the occasion of his Lordship's procession to the Royal Courts of Justice, on Monday, the 9th November, 1891 :—

"To the Right Hon. David Evans,

"Lord Mayor of London,

"Alderman of the Ward of Castle Baynard.

"My Lord Mayor,

"We, the Inhabitants of the Ward of Castle Baynard, take this opportunity to express our hearty congratulations to you, as the Alderman of our Ward, on your having attained the highest dignity to which your fellow Citizens can elect you — namely, the honourable and important position of Lord Mayor of the City of London. In taking upon yourself the onerous duties and responsibilities of this high office you may be sure that you carry with you our best wishes.

"In the ordinary course you would not have been called upon to take up the office of Lord Mayor until next year, but, owing to circumstances which have recently and unexpectedly arisen, you were brought forward as the Alderman next in seniority for election as Chief Magistrate, and we recognise the loyalty and devotion with which you spontaneously, and at inconvenience to yourself, undertook to fill the office of Lord Mayor for the present year. The long service which you have so well rendered to the Corporation of the City of London, first as a Common Councilman, then as an Alderman, and also as a Sheriff of London and Middlesex, is a sufficient guarantee to us that whilst you are Lord Mayor both the Civic Chair and the office of Chief Magistrate will gain in their importance and dignity, and that you will perform the duties which have now devolved upon you in a manner which will do credit and honour, not only to the Corporation, but also to the Empire.

"We are assured, too, that the causes of charity and hospitality, ever renowned at the Mansion House, will not be forgotten by you, assisted as you will be cordially and gracefully by the Lady Mayoress.

"We are, my Lord Mayor,

"Yours very faithfully,

"F. M. Lewis Farrar, Ward Clerk.

"Signed, on behalf of the Inhabitants of the Ward of Castle Baynard, on the 9th day of November, 1891."

The Lord Mayor's Reply.

TO THE INHABITANTS OF THE WARD OF CASTLE BAYNARD.

"Gentlemen,

"I am deeply touched by, and profoundly grateful for, this further proof of your confidence, esteem, and respect, of which I have had already so many evidences, and I receive your congratulations on my attaining the high and dignified office of Lord Mayor as the sincere reflection of your feelings. I can never forget that the position I now have the honour to hold devolves upon me through my election as Alderman of the ancient and important Ward of Castle Baynard, and I am, therefore, fully conscious of my obligations and indebtedness to you. Ever mindful of the great responsibilities I have undertaken, I shall to the best of my ability endeavour to discharge the duties of Chief Magistrate of the City of London as to merit your continued approval and regard.

"I have the honour to be, Gentlemen,

"Your sincere Friend and Servant,

"DAVID EVANS,

"Lord Mayor."

A RECORD

OF

THE STEPS TAKEN BY THE WARD

FOR

THE RECEPTION OF THE LORD MAYOR

On the 9th November, 1891.

WITH A

LIST OF SUBSCRIBERS TO THE DECORATION FUND,

AND

SOME ACCOUNT OF THE WARD.

Compiled by

EDGAR F. JENKINS, C.C.

An Antiquarian Ramble,
in the company of Master John Stow, through the Ward of Castle Baynard.

BY

CHARLES WELCH, F.S.A.,

Librarian to the Corporation of London.

In the earliest times, most of the Wards of London consisted of a soke or manor, belonging to a powerful landowner, from whom the Ward took its name. Castle Baynard Ward was formerly known as the Ward of Richard de Hadstock. At a later period, the Ward was called after the notable building which for many centuries was its pride and glory.

Baynard's Castle.

GLO.—" Go, Lovel, with all speed to Doctor Shaw,—
 Go thou [*to* CATESBY] to Friar Penker; bid them both
 Meet me, within this hour, at Baynard's Castle."
 RIC. III. *Act* 3, *Sc.* 5.

This once eminent building stood on the north bank of the Thames, in Thames Street, and received its name from William Baynard, a nobleman, Lord of Dunmow, who came over with William the Conqueror, and who was its first founder. Fitzstephen, who wrote in the reign of Henry II, notices it in his time as being

a considerable building. "In the west part of the City," says he, "are two most strong castles," of which he specifies this as one. And Gervase of Tilbury, a contemporary author, speaks still more expressly as to its importance. "Two castles are built with walls "and ramparts, whereof one is in right of possession Baynard's, the "other is the Baron Montfitchet's."

The following is a concise outline of the descent of the castle, and its subsequent history. Baynard, the founder, dying in the reign of William Rufus, left it to his son, Geoffry, from whom it came to William Baynard, who, having forfeited his barony of Little Dunmow and "honor of Baynard's Castle," both were conferred by Henry the First on Robert Fitzrichard, the son of Gilbert, Earl of Clare. From this Robert Fitzrichard, by several descents, Baynard's Castle came into the possession of Robert Fitzwalter, a Baron, in the reign of King John; who, having displeased that monarch, he ordered the castle to be demolished, but afterwards gave him permission to re-build it. In 1303, the son of Robert Fitzwalter acknowledged his service to the City of London for his castle of Baynard before Sir John Blount, Mayor, and swore to be true to the liberties of the City. The City, at the same time, recognised a declaration of the rights of the same Robert Fitzwalter, who is therein called "The City's Banner-bearer." Several of the Fitzwalters, after this period, appear to have owned it, till the honor of this residence at length fell from the family, in a way Stow professes himself unable to account for, and came into the possession of the Crown.

In 1428 Baynard's Castle was burnt; and, being re-built by Humphry, Duke of Gloucester, he resided there until his attainder and death in 1446. The next remarkable occupant was, as noticed in the quotation above, Richard, Duke of Gloucester, afterwards Richard III, who assumed the regal title there. From him it came into the possession of Henry VII; who finally re-built it, and occasionally made it the scene of his festivities. From the reign of

Henry VII to that of Edward VI not much notice is taken of Baynard's Castle. About the latter period, probably in consequence of the royal grant, it appears to have been in the possession of the Earls of Pembroke, and was then called "Pembroke House;" and soon afterwards, viz., in 1553, the council assembled here, and proclaimed Mary queen, in opposition to Lady Jane Grey.

The external appearance of Baynard's Castle was rather venerable than grand. A circular tower bounded the south-west corner, with a bell-shaped roof and three windows. Two projections had each windows in two ranges; then a hexagon tower, considerably higher than the roof, with three ranges of windows, some of them being on each side. From that to the eastern end were five projections, each containing two windows in double ranges, and terminating in pointed roofs. At the eastern corner was another hexagon tower, nearly similar to the former one. A large arched gateway towards its east end communicated, by a small bridge and stairs, with the Thames.

The interior was divided into two courtyards, each of which was completely surrounded by buildings, containing the various state and other apartments. To the upper stories of these the ascent was by staircases, winding round circular and hexagonal towers. The south side had its foundations in the river Thames. The north front faced Thames Street, from which was the principal entrance. The whole structure, which, when perfect, covered a very considerable site, was destroyed by the Fire of London, leaving a mere shell. Two of the towers, incorporated with other buildings, remained until the early part of this century, but were pulled down to make room for the buildings of the Carron Iron Company.

The antiquities of the Ward of Castle Baynard are thus quaintly summarised by Stow: "The ornaments of this ward be parish churches "four, of old time a castle, divers noblemen's houses, halls of com- "panies twain, and such others as shall be shown."

Thames Street Mansions.

The south-side of Thames Street formerly contained many notable mansions in ancient times. At the east end stood an ancient mansion called Beaumont's Inn, which belonged to that family of noblemen in the 4th Edward III. Edward IV. in the 5th year of his reign, gave it to his Lord Chamberlain Hastings, Master of his Mints. It afterwards passed into the possession of the Earls of Huntington, and was known as Huntington House. Further west, and beyond Paul's Wharf, was another large house called Scrope's Inn, so named from a former proprietor in the reign of Henry VI. Stow also describes another great messuage in Thames Street, east of Baynard's Castle, formerly belonging to the Abbey of Fiscampe, which came into Edward III's hands after his French campaigns, and was given by that monarch to Sir Simon Burleigh, K.G., and therefore called Burleigh House.

Beside Baynard's Castle formerly stood another tower built by Edward II. Edward III gave it to William, Duke of Hamelake, at a rent of one rose yearly, to be paid for all service. This afterwards became Legate's Inn, but had disappeared in Stow's time, its site being occupied by wood wharves. Puddle Wharf, an ancient water-gate into the Thames, is said by Stow to have been so called from horses watering there, and making puddle with their trampling. In Castle Lane, which has now disappeared, was a large house belonging to the Priory of Oakbourne, in Wiltshire, which was the Prior's residence when he stayed in London. In this lane, too, was a mill or mills belonging to the Templars of the New Temple, who obtained a grant from King John of a site on the Fleet, near Baynard's Castle, to make a mill, and the whole course of the water of the Fleet to serve the same mill. The mill was removed and destroyed in the year 1307, by order of Parliament, upon complaint by Henry Laire, Earl of Lincoln, of "noyances done to the water of the Fleet."

St. Benet's, Paul's Wharf.

Coming back to the east end of Thames Street, and taking now the north side, the first object of interest is the church of St. Benet, over against Paul's Wharf, known also as St. Benet Hude or Hythe. Here were buried Sir William Cheiny, knight, and Margaret, his wife, in 1442, Sir Gilbert Dethick, Garter King-at-Arms, and, at a later date, Inigo Jones, the architect, and several high officers of the neighbouring College of Arms. St. Benet's was united with St. Nicolas Cole Abbey, under the Union of Benefices Act, 1860, but the church was not pulled down. It now belongs to a Welsh congregation, services according to the rites of the Church of England being held every Sunday. West of St. Benet's, at the south end of Addle Street, stood an ancient building belonging to the Lords of Barkly, and called Barkly's Inn. Then, turning to the north, is the parish church of St. Andrew-in-the-Wardrobe, which still exists at the west end of Queen Victoria Street.

The King's Wardrobe.

Close adjoining, formerly stood the King's Great Wardrobe, built by Sir John Beauchamp, Constable of Dover and Warden of the Cinque Ports, who died in 1359 and was buried in St. Paul's Cathedral. His executors sold the house to King Edward III, to whom the parson of St. Andrew's complained that Sir John had pulled down divers houses, to build in their place the same house, wherethrough he was hindered of his accustomed tithes paid by the tenants of old time. The King satisfied the complainant by granting him forty shillings a year out of that house for ever. Richard III made it his residence in the second year of his reign. Secret letters and writings concerning the State were usually enrolled in the King's Wardrobe, and not in the Chancery. On the east side of Peter's Hill formerly stood a large and ancient house belonging to the Abbey of St. Mary in York, and used as the Abbott's town house.

In St. Paul's Wharf Hill, now known as Benet's Hill, on the east side, stood the hall of the Woodmongers' Company, but both the Company and their hall have long since disappeared. Next adjoining is Derby House, now known as

Herald's College.

This ancient body received its first charter of incorporation from Richard III, who gave them, for the residence and assembling of the heralds, Poultney's Inn, "a righte fayre and stately house," in Cold Harbour. They afterwards removed to the hospital of Our Lady of Rounceval at Charing Cross, and finally settled at Derby House, St. Benet's Hill, granted by Queen Mary, in 1555, to Sir Gilbert Dethick, Garter King-at-Arms, and to the other heralds and their successors. The college has, since 1622, consisted of 13 officers—three kings, namely, Garter Principal, Clarencieux, and Norroy; six heralds—Lancaster, Somerset, Richmond, Windsor, York, and Chester; and four poursuivants—Rouge Croix, Blue Mantle, Portcullis, and Blue Dragon. These hold their places by appointment of the Duke of Norfolk, as Hereditary Earl Marshal. In ancient times the duties of the heralds were both varied and important, and included the marshalling and ordering of coronations, marriages, christenings, funerals, interviews, feasts of kings and princes, cavalcades, shows, jousts, tournaments, and combats before the constable and marshal. Another honorable service of the officers-at-arms was the bearing of letters and messages to foreign princes and persons in authority. These officers were the "Chivalers of Arms" or Knights Riders, the original king's messengers, and gave their name to Knightrider Street. The college still retains the sole right to grant arms, and preserves among its records the genealogies of the nobility and gentry. Further north, near the south chain of St. Paul's Churchyard, was the Paul Head Tavern, formerly called Paul's Brewhouse. On the opposite side of the street was Paul's Bakehouse. Both of these establishments were in former days actively employed in ministering to the wants of the officials of the Cathedral.

Doctors' Commons.

On the south side of Knightrider Street was Doctors' Commons, which was a College of Doctors of Civil Law incorporated for the study and practice of Civil Law. The civilians and canonists were formerly lodged in a house subsequently the Queen's Head Tavern in Paternoster Row, whence they removed, in Elizabeth's reign, to a house purchased for them by Dr. Harvey, Dean of the Arches. Here they lived in a collegiate manner and *commoned* together, whence the college was named Doctors' Commons; and the doctors dined together on every court day. This house was destroyed by the Great Fire in 1666, when the college removed to Exeter House, Strand, till the rebuilding of the edifice in Great Knightrider Street in 1672. In Doctors' Commons formerly sat the Court of Arches, the Consistory Court of the Bishop of London, and the High Court of Admiralty. The walls of the college hall above the wainscot were covered with the richly emblazoned coats-of-arms of all the doctors for a century or two past. The College was dissolved about the year 1858, and shortly after the Courts which formerly sat there were removed to Westminster, and the College buildings have been since pulled down.

Blacksmiths' Hall and St. Mary Magdalen's.

In Lambeth Hill, on the west side, formerly stood Blacksmiths' Hall, but the Company have since disposed of its site and no longer possess a hall. On the north side of Knightrider Street, and at the eastern extremity of the ward, is the church of St. Mary Magdalen, which was burnt down in the Great Fire and has recently been again destroyed by fire. With this church was united St. Gregory-by-St. Paul's, a very ancient church, which formerly stood at the south side of the cathedral. Its beautiful marble font is still preserved, but bears traces of the Great Fire. The registers, both of this church and of St. Mary Magdalen, which go back to an early date, very fortunately escaped destruction in both the fires described above. The remains of the church of St. Mary Magdalen, which had but little antiquarian

interest, are about to be pulled down, the parish having been united with St. Martin's, Ludgate. Adjoining the church, on the west side, stood in Stow's time, a conduit or cistern of lead, castellated with stone, for receipt of Thames water, conveyed at the cost of Barnard Randolph, who was buried in St. Mary Magdalen's, in 1583.

The King's Exchange.

By the side of St. Mary Magdalen's church northward, runs Old Change, forming the eastern boundary of the ward, and so called from the King's Exchange, where bullion was minted into coin. Between Knightrider Street and Carter Lane formerly lay Do Little Lane, so called, says Stow, from not being inhabited by artificers or open shopkeepers. Further west is Sermon Lane, a corruption for Shere Moniers' Lane, according to Stow, who explains that the business of the Shere Moniers was to cut or round the plates to be coined or stamped into sterling pence.

College of Physicians.

In Knightrider Street formerly stood the College of Physicians. The College was founded in 1518 by Linacre, physician to Kings Henry VII and Henry VIII, who lived in Knightrider Street, and there received his friends, Erasmus, Latimer and Sir Thomas More. Linacre was the first President of the College, and the members met at his house, which he bequeathed to them; the estate being still the property of the College. Thence they removed to a house in Amen Corner, and, after the Great Fire, a new College was erected by Sir Christopher Wren, in Warwick Lane. Here they remained till 1825, when they finally removed to their present abode in Trafalgar Square and Pall Mall East, which was erected, from designs by Sir Robert Smirke, at a cost of £30,000.

Stationers' Hall.

In the north-west corner of the Ward is Stationers' Hall, situated in Stationers' Hall Court, Ludgate Hill. The Company of Stationers

is one of the few London companies the membership of which is restricted to those practising its own craft, that is, the allied trades of bookselling, stationery, printing, bookbinding, print-selling and engraving. The Company still continue to exercise control over the publishing trade, and also engages in business, as a publishing body, in their corporate capacity. They exercise these powers under a charter granted to them by Charles II in 1684, and confirmed by William and Mary in 1690; but they existed as a fraternity long previous to the introduction of printing. They were first incorporated on the 4th May, 1557, by a charter of Philip and Mary, which was renewed by Elizabeth in 1588. Under their charters, they were empowered to search for and seize obnoxious books; printers were compelled to serve their time under a member of the Company; and every publication, from a Bible to a ballad, was required to be "Entered at Stationers' Hall." The registers of the Stationers' Company date from the beginning of Elizabeth's reign, in 1558, and form an invaluable series of records, in illustration of our national literature. They have been recently made accessible to literary students by the admirable transcript of Professor Arber. The Company has long been noted for the excellent series of almanacs which it publishes; the most important of those now issued is the British Almanac and Companion. Samuel Richardson, the novelist, was Master of the Company in 1754, and his portrait, and those of Prior, Steele, John Bunyan, Bishop Hoadley, William Bowyer, and other notable persons, are preserved in the stock-room. The Company also support and maintain a flourishing public school in Bolt Court, Fleet Street, which accommodates upwards of 300 boys.

The Cathedral and its Precincts.

The Ward of Castle Baynard is further distinguished by comprising within its bounds, at the north and north-east extremity, the grand historic structure of St. Paul's Cathedral, with the several notable

buildings in its precincts, some of which have long since disappeared. It is impossible, in this brief sketch, to do more than mention these by name. They comprise:—Paul's Cross, the Bishop's Palace, with the Lollard's Tower, the Chapter House and Deanery, and the interesting labyrinth of courts and alleys surrounding the cathedral, whose names still re-call the occupations of the text writers and stationers who gained a livelihood by writing and selling various service-books and catechisms for use in the cathedral. They include the far-famed Paternoster Row, Creed Lane, Ave Maria Lane, and Amen Corner.

Some Aldermen of Castle Baynard Ward, With their Companies, Who have served the Office of Lord Mayor.

1453. SIR JOHN NORMAN; *Draper*.
    Introduced the custom of the Lord Mayor going by water to Westminster instead of riding there as before. Alderman of Cheap whilst Mayor.

1457. SIR GEOFFREY BOLEYN; *Mercer*.
    Great-great-grandfather of Queen Elizabeth; ancestor of Admiral Viscount Nelson. Became Alderman of Bassishaw by Prerogative as Lord Mayor.

1465. SIR RALPH VERNEY; *Mercer*.
    Knighted in the field. M.P. for London. Ancestor of Earl Verney.

1481. SIR WILLIAM HERIOT; *Draper*.
    M.P. for London.

1486. SIR HENRY COLET; *Mercer*.
    Father of Dean Colet, who founded St. Paul's School. Alderman of Cornhill whilst Mayor.

1508. Sir STEPHEN JENNINGS; *Draper.*
  Founder of the Wolverhampton Grammar School. Also an eminent member of the Merchant Taylors.

1512. Sir WILLIAM COPINGER; *Fishmonger.*
  Gave half his goods to the poor. Died in his Mayoralty.

1534. Sir JOHN CHAMPNEYS; *Skinner.*
  Alderman of Cordwainer whilst Mayor.

1549. Sir ROWLAND HILL; *Mercer.*
  A very eminent man and a benefactor. Endowed a Grammar School and built many bridges. Alderman of Walbrook whilst Mayor.

1558. Sir THOMAS LEE; *Mercer.*
  Ancestor of Earl of Chatham, William Pitt, and others of the nobility. Alderman of Broad Street whilst Mayor.

1574. Sir JAMES HAWES; *Clothworker.*
  Alderman of Cornhill whilst Mayor.

1583. Sir EDWARD OSBORNE; *Clothworker.*
  Ancestor of the Duke of Leeds. Alderman of Candlewick whilst Mayor.

1592. Sir WILLIAM ROWE; *Ironmonger.*

1611. Sir JAMES PEMBERTON; *Goldsmith.*
  Alderman of Bishopsgate whilst Mayor.

1619. Sir WILLIAM COCKAIGNE; *Skinner.*
  First Governor of the Irish Society. His son was created Viscount Cullen. Alderman of Lime Street whilst Mayor.

1637. Sir RICHARD FENN; *Haberdasher.*

Some Aldermen of Castle Baynard Ward.

1666. Sir WILLIAM BOLTON; *Merchant Taylor.*

1668. Sir WILLIAM TURNER; *Merchant Taylor.*
At one time Alderman of Farringdon Within, afterwards of Candlewick. Founder of a Grammar School, and a great benefactor.

1705. Sir THOMAS RAWLINSON; *Vintner.*

1717. Sir WILLIAM LEWEN; *Haberdasher.*
M.P. for Poole, Dorsetshire.

1732. JOHN BARBER; *Goldsmith.*
A printer, of great fame in his day. A friend of Bolingbroke, Pope and Swift, to whom he bequeathed money.

1747. Sir ROBERT LADBROKE; *Grocer.*
M.P. for London. President of Christ's Hospital. Became Alderman of Bridge Without after he had passed the chair.

1778. SAMUEL PLUMBE; *Goldsmith.*

1791. Sir JOHN HOPKINS; *Grocer.*

1810. JOSHUA JONATHAN SMITH; *Ironmonger.*

1838. SAMUEL WILSON; *Weaver.*
Colonel of the City of London Militia. Created a Trust Fund to provide a ring for each succeeding Alderman of Castle Baynard who should become Lord Mayor. Became Alderman of Bridge Without after he had passed the chair.

1871. Sir SILLS JOHN GIBBONS, Bart.; *Salter.*

1891. DAVID EVANS; *Haberdasher.*

Note as to the Aldermen.

Prior to 1700 no official calendar was made of Aldermen who became Lord Mayor, so that it has been impossible, in the short time allowed for the preparation of this volume, to give a full list of the Aldermen of Castle Baynard who became Chief Magistrate. In former times it was no uncommon thing for Aldermen to be translated from one Ward to another. This fact has added greatly to the difficulty of tracing the Mayoralty of many Aldermen. Why this practice obtained it is not quite known. It may have been because the office of Mayor came in rotation of Wards, and not, as in later times, in order of seniority of the Aldermen, and that the Alderman of the Ward whose turn it was to be Lord Mayor, not being willing or able to accept the office, he obtained a substitute as it were of a brother Alderman from another Ward to take his place, to save himself the fine for non-acceptance of the office. During the troublous reigns it was very difficult to find citizens who would serve either as Alderman or as Lord Mayor, and many translations and changes between Aldermen occurred to avoid the higher office. Since 1700, however, a different state of things has been in practice. Translations have become quite the exception and not the rule, consequently it has been easy to trace the career of an Alderman after his election. Accordingly, an official list has been made of all the Aldermen living in 1700, and since elected, with their Wards, and the dates of their election as Sheriff and as Lord Mayor. It will be a surprise to many to learn that during the past and present centuries no less than ten out of the fifteen Aldermen elected for the Ward of Castle Baynard have occupied the Civic Chair, and that no other Ward can show a greater number of Lord Mayors during the same period, whilst there are 19 Wards (excluding Bridge Without) which have not had so many.

Note as to the Aldermen.

The following Table will be interesting :—

Ward.	Aldermen living in 1700 and since elected.	Lord Mayors.
Castle Baynard	15	10
Billingsgate	13	10
Cornhill	11	10
Cripplegate	10	10
Langbourn	10	10
Walbrook	15	10
Bishopsgate	12	9
Dowgate	13	9
Portsoken	14	9
Queenhithe	18	9
Candlewick	11	9
Vintry	12	9
Aldersgate	12	8
Aldgate	15	8
Broad Street	14	8
Coleman Street	14	8
Cordwainer ...	16	8
Farringdon Within	13	8
Farringdon Without	13	8
Tower	12	8
Bread Street	12	7
Bridge ...	16	7
Cheap ...	17	7
Lime Street	17	7
Bassishaw	14	5
*Bridge Without ...	2	1

* Bridge Without is practically the Bailiwick of Southwark. The Ward is represented only by its Alderman, who used to be nominated and elected by the Court of Aldermen. In 1711, however, an Act of Common Council was passed whereby the Ward, on a vacancy arising, was to be offered to those Aldermen who had passed the Chair according to seniority. By another Act of Common Council, passed in 1725, the election of an Alderman of Bridge Without is vested in the Common Council. Twice, viz., in 1758 and 1853, Aldermen of Castle Baynard, after having passed the Chair, have become Aldermen of Bridge Without.

Note as to the Aldermen.

It is not unreasonable to infer, from the above table, that during the earlier years of the Mayoralty, Castle Baynard enjoyed the privilege of having a good average number of Aldermen who served the office of Lord Mayor; although, for reasons already given, it has not been possible to show a complete list of such Aldermen prior to 1700.

The present year is the 703rd of the Mayoralty of the City of London. Allowing for those who served in the office for more than one year, and also for such as may have died during their Mayoralty (when a second appointment in the same year had to be made), Mr. Alderman Evans is the 590th citizen who has filled the office. Long may the Civic Chair of the ancient City of London find a worthy occupant, and may Castle Baynard ever, as during the present year, have an Alderman "ready, aye, ready," to become Lord Mayor!

Lord Mayors of London having a Welsh lineage.

It would be interesting if a complete list of Lord Mayors having a Welsh lineage could be given here. The result of a search and of a somewhat careful enquiry shows, however, that this cannot be done. It is not improbable that several of those who filled the Civic Chair had a Welsh ancestry, but if so, their nationality had become changed from the fact that their more immediate ancestors had left the Principality and permanently taken up their abode in England and so abandoned their Welsh domicile. There appear to be only three who, having themselves come from Wales to seek their fortune in London, became Lord Mayor. These are :—

Sir THOMAS EXMEWE ; *Goldsmith*.
> Lord Mayor 1517. Alderman of Cripplegate, who came from Flintshire.

Sir JAMES YARDFORD ; *Mercer*.
> Lord Mayor 1579. Alderman of Candlewick, who came from Kidwylly, Carmarthenshire.

Right Hon. DAVID EVANS, F.R.G.S. ; *Haberdasher*.
> Lord Mayor 1891. Alderman of Castle Baynard, who was born at Llantrisant, Glamorganshire ; son of Thomas Evans, of Glan Muchudd, Llantrisant.

The following are instances of Lord Mayors of Welsh descent whose parents or grandparents had left the Principality and settled in England before they took office :—

Sir WILLIAM HUMPHREYS, Bart. ; *Ironmonger*.
> Lord Mayor 1714 (a Londoner). Grandson of William ap Humphrey of Penrhin, Montgomeryshire. Entertained King George I, with the Prince and Princess of Wales, at his Mayoralty Dinner at Guildhall. M.P. for Marlborough.

Welsh Lineage.

Sir RICHARD GLYN, Bart.; *Salter.*
    Lord Mayor 1758 (a Surreyman). Grandson of William Glyn, of Glyn Llyvon, Caernarvonshire. M.P. for Coventry.

Sir RICHARD CARR GLYN, Bart.; *Salter.*
    Lord Mayor 1798 (a Surreyman). Son of the above. Father of the first Lord Wolverton. M.P. for St. Ives.

A Welsh extraction has also been claimed for the following:—

Andrew Aubrey	*Mayor*	1339, 1340, 1351.
Sir Bartilmew James	,,	1479 (? Londoner).
Sir Francis Jones	,,	1620 (? Salopian).
Sir Thomas Davies	,,	1676 (? Londoner).
Sir James Edwards	,,	1678 (? Yorkshireman).
Sir William Pritchard	,,	1683 (? Surreyman).
Sir John Williams	,,	1735 (? Londoner).
Sir Samuel Pennant	,,	1748 (? Londoner).
Sir Watkin Lewes	,,	1780 (? Londoner).
Sir Charles Price, Bart.	,,	1802 (? Surreyman).
Robert Waithman	,,	1823 (Born at Wrexham).

It may be added that Rowland Haylin, who was Sheriff in 1624, caused the Bible to be translated into Welsh, so that there is reason to suppose that he may have been of Welsh descent.

In this connection it is interesting to note that the British and Foreign Bible Society, whose habitat is in Castle Baynard Ward, and whose output for 1890 exceeded 850,000 Bibles, and 1,346,000 New Testaments, besides upwards of 1,728,000 separate books or portions of Scripture, and whose income for the year was £217,148, owes its origin to Mary Jones, a little Welsh maid. Her memory is kept green in the Library of the Society by the exhibition of her Bible, which bears this inscription:—

    "The Bible of Mary Jones, of Brynerug, whose journey to the Rev. Thomas Charles, in Bala, for the purchase of it in 1800, led to the foundation of the Bible Society in 1804."

Alderman Wilson's Bequest.

A very interesting and unique Trust for the benefit of the Aldermen of Castle Baynard who should become Lord Mayor was created in 1865 by Colonel Samuel Wilson, late an esteemed Alderman of the Ward, who served the office of Lord Mayor with remarkable brilliancy and success. The late Samuel Wilson and his family were for many years commercially connected with the City of London, and in the year 1833 he was elected Alderman of the Ward of Castle Baynard. He was subsequently unanimously elected by the Livery in Common Hall to fill the office of Sheriff of London and Middlesex, and in the year 1838 he served the office of Lord Mayor. At the conclusion of his year of office as Lord Mayor he was presented by the public with plate of the value of £1,500 in testimony of their estimation of the manner in which he had maintained the dignity, hospitality, and efficiency of his high office. The worthy Alderman bequeathed the whole of this plate upon Trust for the use of the Lord Mayor for the time being at the Mansion House. In the Trust Deed executed by him in 1865, he expressed himself as having "a deep-rooted attachment to "the free institutions of the ancient City of London, and an affectionate "regard for his brothers of the Court of Aldermen, for the Members "and Officers of the Corporation, and for the Ward of Castle Baynard, "after an intimate, friendly, and official connection existing between "them for more than 34 years, and being desirous to leave behind him "an enduring memorial of those feelings," he determined to invest the sum of £4,000 in the names of Trustees, whom he appointed, to be

the two senior Aldermen, the Recorder, and the City Chamberlain, for the time being. The income of this fund was directed by the worthy Alderman to be applied in the manner more particularly stated by him, but as to a part of it with directions that a sum of £100 should be set aside by the Trustees and held by them upon the Trust following :—

"And as to the sum of £100 hereinbefore directed to be set aside, the same "shall be invested by the Trustees until the Alderman of Castle Baynard Ward "shall be elected Lord Mayor of London, and when and so often as such event "shall happen the said sum shall be applied in the purchase of a ring to be pre-"sented by the Chamberlain of the said City of London for the time being in the "Guildhall of the said City to the said Lord Mayor elect immediately after he "shall have taken the usual oaths of office."

Mr. Alderman David Evans, the present Lord Mayor, is the first recipient of this ring, he being the first Alderman of the Ward of Castle Baynard who has become entitled thereto under the terms of the Trust. The ring was presented to him by the Chamberlain, in Common Hall on Saturday, the 7th November, 1891. It is of 18-carat gold, with a superb diamond in the centre. The design represents the City dragons modelled in full relief, holding in their claws and teeth the diamond. Resting upon the backs of the dragons, and between their wings, are miniature coats of arms, one of the City of London, and the other of the Lord Mayor, enamelled in heraldic colours. Inside the ring is inscribed, "Presented to David Evans, Lord Mayor of London, 1891, under Alderman Samuel Wilson's Trust."

Assistance of
Dean and Chapter of St. Paul's Cathedral,
and of the Richmond Herald.

Application having been made to the Dean and Chapter of St. Paul's for permission to erect the Model Baynard Castle within the boundary line of the Cathedral yard, the following cordial reply was given by the Dean :—

                         "Deanery,
                            "St. Paul's, E.C.,
                                  "*10th October, 1891.*

"My dear Sir,

    "I gladly accord the consent of the Dean and Chapter to your erecting a "Model of Baynard Castle upon the ground at the west front of the Cathedral, for the "9th November.

                        "Yours very truly,
                            "ROBT. GREGORY,
"Edgar F. Jenkins, Esq."   "*Dean.*

With the permission of Mr. Athil, the Richmond Herald at the College of Arms, his assistant, Mr. Eve, kindly provided coloured sketches from which some of the shields placed on the model Baynard Castle were copied.

Model Baynard Castle.

Copied from Sketch in the "City Press."

The Address being read to the Lord Mayor.

Model Baynard Castle.

From Sketch by Mr. Walter Mills, of the Firm of Messrs. Pain & Son, St. Mary Axe, the Contractors for the Decorations.

Shields placed on the Model Baynard Castle.

THE LORD MAYOR.

MR. DEPUTY BROWN, C.C.

MR. EDGAR F. JENKINS, C.C.

Shields on the Model Castle Baynard.

THE CORPORATION OF THE CITY OF LONDON.

THE DEAN AND CHAPTER OF
ST. PAUL'S CATHEDRAL.

THE CORPORATION OF
HERALD'S COLLEGE.

Decorations on Ludgate Hill.

Decorations in St. Paul's Churchyard.

Copied from Sketch in the "City Press."

The "Times,"

of 10th November, 1891, contained the following description of the Decorations in the Ward:—

"In the Lord Mayor's ward, Castle Baynard, much had been done to show him honour. Last month, at a meeting of the inhabitants, a committee was appointed to collect funds for decorating the chief streets in the ward through which the procession would pass—Upper Thames Street, Queen Victoria Street, St. Paul's Churchyard, and Ludgate Hill. A sufficient response was made to the appeal, and Messrs. Pain and Son, the firework makers, undertook to provide what was needed. In the result a large number of banners were put up, all bearing appropriate inscriptions. Among these were the following:—At St. Peter's Hill, where the procession entered the ward, 'Castle Baynard greets you'; at the corner of Old Change, 'The Ward wishes its Alderman happiness and prosperity'; on Ludgate Hill, at the boundary of the ward, '.Au revoir.' Queen Victoria Street was crossed by strings of streamers; Venetian masts and festoons of flowers lined each side, and some of the houses hung out flags. The sight in St. Paul's Churchyard must have taken not a few by surprise, the begrimed walls being relieved at intervals round the railings by Venetian masts, festoons of flowers, and trophies of flags and shields. But the most important part of the work has yet to be mentioned. South of the statue of Queen Anne was a large model of Baynard Castle, from which the name of the ward is taken. Built by one of William the Conqueror's companions, this fortress, after more than one change of ownership, became a sort of Royal Palace, and many scenes of historic interest were enacted within its walls. Here, for example, the Duke of Buckingham offered the Crown to Gloucester—an incident which Shakespere has faithfully followed in *Richard III.*— and here Henry VII received many of his ambassadors. It went down in the Great Fire, its last tenant being the Countess of Pembroke. The model had over its portcullis the arms and crest of the Lord Mayor, with the arms of the two corporations within the ward—the Dean and Chapter of St. Paul's and Herald's College—on either side. The shield of the Corporation of the City of London appeared on the east, and those of the two senior members of the Court of Common Council for the ward, Mr. Deputy Brown and Mr. Edgar F. Jenkins, on the west. The model was designed chiefly from a drawing in the possession of Mr. Jenkins, at whose suggestion it is understood to have been put up. On reaching the spot yesterday the Lord Mayor stopped for a few seconds to receive the following address":—

[*Here followed the address and reply.*]

The "Evening Standard,"

of 11th November, 1891, contained the following description of the Decorations in the Ward:—

"Castle Baynard Ward, through which the procession passed, was nicely decorated, under the direction of the Committee appointed at a meeting of the inhabitants, to collect funds for the purpose. A liberal response was made to the appeal of the Committee, and Messrs. Pain and Sons, the well-known pyrotechnists, were entrusted with the work of carrying out the decorations, no expense being spared in this effort to do honour to the Lord Mayor. At St. Peter's Hill, where the Lord Mayor and his procession first entered the Ward, was a pretty design, with the words 'Castle Baynard greets you.' After leaving Upper Thames Street, the procession entered the lower half of Queen Victoria Street, where large crowds had for some hours previously been standing awaiting its appearance. Each side of the street was lined with Venetian masts, from which hung festoons of flowers. Strings of streamers crossed the street, and nearly every business establishment hung out flags and banners. Several mottoes in Welsh were displayed, and one large cloth hanging across the street brought boldly into view the inscription, 'Welcome to our 'Alderman and Lord Mayor.' The shop windows were filled with spectators, and a large platform erected in front of St. Anne's Church was reserved for the children of Castle Baynard, Queenhithe, and Vintry Ward Schools. Leaving Victoria Street at the junction with Cannon Street, the procession turned into the latter thoroughfare, where the footpaths were lined with people. Cannon Street was gaily bedecked with bunting, and at Old Change there was displayed a scarlet cloth, containing in large letters the sentiment, 'The Ward wishes its Alderman happiness and prosperity.' The decorations in St. Paul's Churchyard were very effective. At intervals all round the churchyard Venetian masts were placed, bearing trophies of flags and shields, whilst from mast to mast stretched festoons of flowers. Flags and banners were displayed in profusion from the windows of the large business establishments in the Churchyard,

Extract from "Evening Standard."

which was filled with people, the steps of St. Paul's Cathedral forming a most convenient standpoint. Here, again, the handiwork of the Committee of Castle Baynard was seen to great advantage. Acting on the suggestion of Mr. Edgar F. Jenkins, one of the senior representatives of the Ward of Castle Baynard, the Committee decided to erect a large model of the old Baynard Castle, from which the Ward takes its name. The model, excellently designed, occupied a prominent position close to Queen Anne's statue. Over the portcullis appeared the Arms and Crest of the Lord Mayor, flanked on either side by the Arms of the two Corporations within the Ward, namely, those of the Dean and Chapter of St. Paul's and of the Herald's College. The Shield of the Corporation of the City of London is fixed on the east side of the model, whilst those of Mr. Deputy Brown and Mr. Edgar F. Jenkins, as the two senior members of the Ward, are placed on the west side. The members of the Common Council for the Ward, wearing their robes, assembled within the model castle, and when the procession reached this point there was a temporary halt, made for the purpose of enabling Mr. Anderson, on behalf of the deputation representing the inhabitants of the Ward, to present the Lord Mayor with the appended Address."

[*Here followed the address and reply.*]

Proceedings of a Preliminary Meeting

of the Members of the Court of Common Council of the Castle Baynard Ward, held on the 21st September, 1891.

At a Meeting of the Common Councilmen of the Ward of Castle Baynard, convened by circular, re the election of Lord Mayor, and held at the Ward Clerk's Office, on the 21st September, 1891,

Mr. DEPUTY BROWN, C.C., in the Chair.

* * * * * *

The Deputy referred to the approaching election of Lord Mayor, and suggested that steps should be taken to show proper honor to Mr. Alderman Evans in the event of his being elected to fill the high and important office.

Mr. Edgar F. Jenkins, C.C., moved,

Mr. Alexander Ritchie, C.C., seconded, and

It was unanimously resolved—

"That in view of the approaching election of Mr. Alderman Evans to the "office of Lord Mayor for the ensuing year, it is desirable that the Ward "be decorated on the 9th November next, and that a Reception Com- "mittee for the Ward be appointed, and that a Ward meeting be called "to give effect to this resolution."

Fac-Simile of Notice

Convening a Public Meeting of the Inhabitants and Ratepayers of the Ward.

CASTLE BAYNARD WARD.

TAKE NOTICE that a public meeting of the Inhabitants and Ratepayers of this Ward will be held at the Blackfriars Infant School, No. 13, St. Andrew's Hill, Blackfriars, on Tuesday, the 6th of October next, at 12 o'clock at Noon precisely:

To consider and resolve upon the steps to be taken to decorate the Ward and to present an address to Mr. Alderman Evans, on the 9th of November next, on the occasion of his entering upon the office of Lord Mayor, and to appoint a Committee to give effect to the above on behalf of the Inhabitants of the Ward.

Dated 29th September, 1891.

F. W. LEWIS FARRAR,
WARD CLERK.

Proceedings at the Public Meeting.

CASTLE BAYNARD WARD.

At a Meeting of the Inhabitants and Ratepayers of the Ward, held on the 6th day of October, 1891, at the Blackfriars Infant School, St. Andrew's Hill, to consider and resolve upon the steps to be taken to decorate the Ward and present an Address to Mr. Alderman Evans, on the 9th November next, on the occasion of his entering on the office of Lord Mayor, and to appoint a Committee to give effect to the above on behalf of the inhabitants of the Ward.

Mr. DEPUTY BROWN, C.C., in the Chair.

The Ward Clerk read the notice convening the meeting.

The Deputy explained the object of the meeting.

Mr. Edgar F. Jenkins, C.C., moved,

Mr. Fydell Rogers seconded, and

It was carried unanimously:—

"That in the opinion of this meeting of Inhabitants and Ratepayers of Castle Baynard Ward, a warm and hearty Reception should be given, and an Address presented, to the Lord Mayor elect, Mr. Alderman Evans, the esteemed Alderman of this Ward, on the 9th November next, when he will pass through the Ward as Lord Mayor, and that a Committee be formed to give effect to this resolution."

Proceedings at the Public Meeting.

Mr. G. T. Thornes, C.C., moved,

Mr. T. J. Douglass seconded, and

It was carried unanimously—

"That the following be the Reception Committee, with power to add to their number:—

Mr. Deputy Brown, C.C.
Alderman Sir Reginald Hanson, Bart., M.P.
Sir G. H. Chubb.
Edgar F. Jenkins, C.C.
George Thistle Thornes, C.C.
Arthur B. Hudson, C.C.
J. C. Chubb, C.C.
William Porter, C.C.
Charles V. Hunter, C.C.
Alexander Ritchie, C.C.
Frederick Cook.
G. Williams.
J. Bignell.
J. R. Fydell Rogers.
T. Newton.
W. Curling Anderson.
Stafford Northcote.

M. Goldstein.
W. H. Making.
H. L. Evans.
R. T. Shrigley.
Key Hardy.
F. Balfour.
T. Drew.
H. O'Brien.
T. J. Douglass.
T. Andrews.
J. Shaw.
A. W. Hurrell.
C. J. Crickmer.
Leonard Fawell.
J. Williams.
William Adamson.
George Thomson."

The proceedings of the Meeting were ordered to be advertised in the *City Press*.

Proceedings of the Reception Committee.

At a Meeting of the Committee held at the Ward Clerk's Office, on the 9th October, 1891.

Mr. DEPUTY BROWN, C.C., in the Chair.

After a resolution inviting Tenders from five eminent firms (named) with a colored sketch for decorating the route of the Procession through the Ward on the 9th November next, had been carried,

Mr. E. F. Jenkins, C.C., moved,

Mr. R. Hirst seconded, and

It was resolved unanimously—

> "That the above firms be requested to furnish a separate special tender and design for a structure representing the Baynard Castle on the four sides, with a portcullis structure to be used by the Reception Committee, from which to present an address to the Lord Mayor, such erection to be placed within the granite posts now existing on the pavement near Queen Anne's Statue, and that the prominent decoration of the Castle be the Welsh Standard, the Arms of the Lord Mayor Elect, the City Arms, the College of Heralds' Arms, and the Cathedral Arms."

At a Meeting of the Committee held at the Ward Clerk's Office, on the 9th October, 1891.

Mr. DEPUTY BROWN, C.C., in the Chair.

Tenders for the decoration of the Ward, and for the Baynard Castle structure having been received from four of the firms who had been invited to tender, and the same having been considered,

Mr. E. F. Jenkins, C.C., moved,

Mr. Fred. Cook seconded, and

It was unanimously resolved—

> "That the tender of Messrs. James Pain and Sons, for the decoration of the ward, and erection of the Castle be accepted."

* * * * * * *

Mr. Fred. Cook moved,

Mr. G. T. Thornes, C.C., seconded, and

It was unanimously resolved—

"That the Deputy with Mr. E. F. Jenkins, C.C., Mr. A. B. Hudson, C.C., Mr. C. V. Hunter, C.C., and Mr. J. C. Chubb, C.C., be appointed a Committee to see the decorations properly carried out."

Mr. E. F. Jenkins, C.C., moved,

Mr. G. T. Thornes, C.C., seconded, and

It was unanimously resolved—

"That it be referred to Mr. Deputy Brown, C.C., Mr. Stafford Northcote, Mr. Frederick Cook, Mr. J. R. Fydell Rogers, and Mr. E. F. Jenkins, C.C., to prepare the draft of the Address to be presented to the Lord Mayor for the approval of the Committee at its next meeting."

Mr. E. F. Jenkins, C.C., moved,

Mr. T. J. Douglass seconded, and

It was unanimously carried -

"That the Address, the Lord Mayor's reply, together with the Minutes of the proceedings of this Committee, including a list of the Subscribers to the Decoration Fund, be bound in Morocco or Russian leather, under the direction of the Sub-Committee appointed to draft the Address, and that the same be presented to the Lord Mayor at the Ward Mote on 21st December next."

The following gentlemen volunteered to canvass for subscriptions, namely—

Mr. Douglass.	Mr. Porter, C.C.
Mr. Thomson.	Mr. Stafford Northcote.
Mr. Adamson.	Mr. Hudson, C.C.
Mr. Hirst.	Mr. Hunter, C.C.
Mr. Making.	Mr. Chubb, C.C.
Mr. Evans.	Mr. Price.
Mr. Thornes, C.C.	Mr. Goldstein.

Proceedings of the Reception Committee.

Mr. E. F. Jenkins, C.C., moved,

Mr. T. J. Douglass seconded, and

It was unanimously resolved—

> "That an Account be opened at the City Bank, Ludgate Hill, to be entitled 'The Castle Baynard Ward Decoration Fund,' and that all money be paid in by each collector to such Account, and that the Deputy and the Ward Clerk be authorised to draw on such account."

Mr. E. F. Jenkins, C.C., moved,

Mr. W. Adamson seconded, and

It was unanimously resolved—

> "That Mr. Fred. Cook, and Mr. J. R. Fydell Rogers be requested to be, and are hereby appointed, the Honorary Auditors of the Fund."

At a Meeting of the Reception Committee, held at the Ward Clerk's Office, on the 6th November, 1891.

Mr. DEPUTY BROWN, C.C., in the Chair.

Mr. E. F. Jenkins, C.C., read the draft Address.

Mr. T. J. Douglass moved,

Mr. R. Hirst seconded, and

It was resolved unanimously—

> "That the draft Address be approved, and that a fair copy thereof be signed by the Ward Clerk on behalf of the Inhabitants of the Ward."

Mr. A. B. Hudson, C.C., moved,

Mr. A. Ritchie, C.C., seconded, and

It was carried unanimously—

> "That Mr. W. Curling Anderson be requested to read the Address to the Lord Mayor, on the 9th inst., from the gateway of the Model Baynard Castle."

Mr. Anderson expressed his pleasure in acceding to this request.

Proceedings of the Reception Committee.

Mr. R. Hirst moved,

Mr. H. L. Evans seconded, and

It was carried unanimously—

"That the following gentlemen do form a Deputation, on behalf of the Ward, "to attend at the Model Baynard Castle, on the reading of the "Address to the Lord Mayor, on the 9th inst. :—

W. Curling Anderson, (to read the Address.)	Stafford Northcote.
	Rowland Hirst.
Edgar F. Jenkins, C.C.	T. J. Douglass.
Arthur B. Hudson, C.C.	George Thomson.
J. C. Chubb, C.C.	William Adamson.
William Porter, C.C.	H. L. Evans.
Charles Val. Hunter, C.C.	Key Hardy.
Alexander Ritchie, C.C.	W. Making.
The Ward Clerk (F. W. Lewis Farrar).	M. Goldstein.
	W. B. Doubleday."
J. R. Fydell Rogers.	

It was suggested and arranged that the Members of the Court of Common Council of the Ward included in the above Deputation should attend in their Mazarine gowns, and that such Members of the Deputation as are entitled to wear Livery gowns should attend in such gowns on the reading of the Address to the Lord Mayor.

Mr. Deputy Brown, C.C., and Mr. George Thistle Thornes, C.C., explained that they could not be appointed on the Deputation, as they would have to attend to their duties as Members of the Lord Mayor and Sheriffs' Committee on same day at Guildhall.

Proceedings of the Decoration Sub-Committee.

WARD CLERK'S OFFICE,
23rd October, 1891.

At a Meeting of the Decoration Sub-Committee, appointed at the Meeting held on the 16th October, 1891,

Mr. DEPUTY BROWN, C.C., in the Chair.

Mr. E. F. Jenkins, C.C., moved,

Mr. A. B. Hudson, C.C., seconded, and

It was unanimously resolved:—

"That, at St. Peter's Hill, across Upper Thames Street, a Banner be placed, "with the following motto:—
"'BAYNARD CASTLE GREETS YOU.'"

"That, at St. Andrew's Hill, across Queen Victoria Street, a Banner be placed, "with the motto:—
"'WELCOME TO OUR ALDERMAN AND LORD MAYOR.'"

"That, at Old Change, across Cannon Street, there be a Banner, with the "motto:—
"'THE WARD WISHES ITS ALDERMAN HAPPINESS AND PROSPERITY.'"

"That, at Ave Maria Lane, across Ludgate Hill, there be a Banner with "the motto:—
"'AU REVOIR.'"

Proceedings of the Address Sub-Committee.

At a Meeting of the Address Sub-Committee held at the Ward Clerk's Office, on 23rd October, 1891.

Mr. DEPUTY BROWN, C.C., in the Chair.

The Form of Address to be presented to the Lord Mayor was considered and agreed to, subject to some few alterations.

At a Meeting of the Address Sub-Committee held at the Ward Clerk's Office, on the 20th November, 1891.

Mr. DEPUTY BROWN, C.C., in the Chair.

The draft of this volume was read and approved of, and instructions were given as to its printing and binding.

At a Meeting of the Members of the Address Sub-Committee, held on the 2nd December, 1891, at 16, Godliman Street.

Mr. DEPUTY BROWN C.C., in the Chair.

Mr. J. R. Fydell Rogers moved,

Mr. Fred. Cook seconded, and

It was carried unanimously—

"That the expense of this Book do not exceed the amount of the balance "at the disposal of the Committee."

Mr. Fred. Cook moved,

Mr. Stafford Northcote seconded, and

It was carried unanimously—

> "That Messrs. Blades, East and Blades be entrusted with the printing of
> "the Book—they to supply 60 copies: one bound in Russia leather,
> "one bound in Morocco, and 58 bound in Roxburgh covers, with all
> "illustrations coloured."

Mr. Alfred F. Blades and Mr. G. Rowland Blades attended the Committee on behalf of their Firm, and accepted the terms of the foregoing Resolution.

Proceedings of the Meetings of Collectors.

WARD CLERK'S OFFICE,
28th October, 1891.

At a Meeting of the Collectors appointed at the meeting held on 16th October, 1891.

Mr. DEPUTY BROWN, C.C., in the Chair.

Reports as to the Funds collected were received from Mr. Douglass, Mr. Adamson, Mr. Making, Mr. Northcote, Mr. Evans, Mr. Hudson, C.C., Mr. Porter, C.C., Mr. Hirst, Mr. Goldstein, and Mr. Thornes, C.C.

The Ward Clerk reported as to the Bank balance.

At a further Meeting of the Collectors, held at the Ward Clerk's Office, on 3rd November, 1891.

Mr. DEPUTY BROWN, C.C., in the Chair.

The Ward Clerk produced the Pass Book of "The Castle Baynard Decoration Fund" and reported thereon.

Reports as to collection of the Fund were also received from Mr. Hirst, Mr. Adamson, Mr. Evans, Mr. Northcote, Mr. Douglass, Mr. Making, Mr. Thornes, C.C.

Fac-Simile of Notice
Convening the Wardmote on 21st December, 1891.

CASTLE BAYNARD WARD.

8th December, 1891.

Sir,

By virtue of a PRECEPT from the RIGHT HON. THE LORD MAYOR, you are hereby required by the RIGHT HONORABLE THE LORD MAYOR, the Right Worshipful DAVID EVANS, Alderman of this Ward, to make your personal appearance at a WARDMOTE, to be holden before him, at the BLACKFRIARS INFANT SCHOOL, No. 13, St. Andrew's Hill, on Monday, the 21st instant, at ELEVEN o'clock in the forenoon precisely, for the purpose of electing WARD OFFICERS for the year ensuing. Hereof fail not.

WILLIAM HALE JEACOCKE,
WARD BEADLE.

NOTE.—It is intended at this Wardmote to present to the Lord Mayor a bound volume, containing the Address of the Inhabitants read to his Lordship on the 9th of November last.

Proceedings at the Wardmote.

CASTLE BAYNARD WARD,
Monday, 21st December, 1891.

At a Wardmote held this day, pursuant to the foregoing notice, the Right Hon. the Lord Mayor attended in State. The Members of the Ward in the Court of Common Council attending in their Mazarine gowns.

THE RIGHT HON. THE LORD MAYOR (the Right Worshipful DAVID EVANS, Alderman of this Ward) in the Chair.

After the business of the Wardmote, Mr. DEPUTY BROWN, C.C., in the name, and on behalf of, the Inhabitants of the Ward in general, and on behalf of the Subscribers to the Decorations on Lord Mayor's Day in particular, presented this Volume, bound in Russia leather, to the Right Hon. the Lord Mayor, the esteemed Alderman of this Ward.

The Proceedings of the Wardmote were ordered to be advertised in the *City Press*.

NOTE.—Subsequently, this Volume, bound in Morocco, was presented to the LADY MAYORESS on behalf of the Subscribers.

Castle Baynard Ward Decoration Fund.

LIST OF SUBSCRIBERS.

Aitchison Brothers
William Adamson
Edward William Allen
Allhausen & Co.
Arthur & Co.
G. Atkinson
Bagshawe Brothers & Co.
Bantoft, Howard & Co.
Thomas Barge
Robert Henry Barnes
James Beavan
Belcher & Ullmer
Robert Smith Bendall
William Birt
Bishop and Clark
Blackfriars Cold Storage Co., Limited
Wm. Blackwood & Son
Brown, Brough & Co.
Deputy William Thornburgh Brown, C.C.
Walter Campbell
Carron Company
Castell Brothers
George Thomas Case
Chapple, Welch & Chapple
Civil Service Supply Association, Limited

H. J. & T. Child
Chubb & Sons.
Sir George H. Chubb.
John Charles Chubb, C.C.
Arthur Coles
Collier & Co.
Cook, Son & Co.
Cornell, Lyell & Co.
George Crabb
Croggon & Co., Limited
Crickmer & Co.
Crute & Son
Davidson & Sons, Ltd.
Dakin & Co.
C. W. Davis
Daires & Sons
T. S. Davy & Sons
Doubleday, Son & Co.
Thomas Joseph Douglass
George Doyle
The Drapers' Record
Wm. Edwards & Son
J. Esson
H. L. Evans
A. Evans
Evans, Hallewell & Co.
A. W. Faber & Co.
F. W. Lewis Farrar

Farquhar & Co., Limited
J. F. Farwig & Co.
Leonard Fawell
Charles William Fink
Frankau, Adolph & Co.
F. S.
Finch
A Friend
Frederick Gill
Globe Parcels Express Company, Limited
Martin Goldstein
Frederick Evelyn Green
Very Rev. Robert Gregory, D.D. (Dean of St. Paul's)
David Gunnell
James Hamilton
Alderman Sir Reginald Hanson, Bart., M.P.
Key Hardy
Sir John Hassard
Alfred Heales
Members of Heralds' College (per W. H. Weldon)
Hilton, Anderson & Co.
Rowland Hirst

Castle Baynard Ward Decoration Fund.

LIST OF SUBSCRIBERS—continued.

Hitchcock, Williams & Co.
George Holden & Son
Holloway & Sharpe
Hope Foundry Company
The Rev. Edgar Hoskins
J. Howell & Co., Limited
Howse, Mead & Co.
Arthur Byrne Hudson, C.C.
Charles Valentine Hunter, C.C.
Hutchins & Co.
Wm. Saunders Cooper Jacob
Edgar Francis Jenkins, C.C.
John Jennings
B. L. Jones & Co.
Thomas Keeble
Keen & Rogers
Max Krause
Franz Frederick Christian Krolle
Walter Bolingbroke Lawrence
Lawry & Upton
Harry Wilmot Lee
Linoleum Company
William John Little
Longman, Green & Co.
Lockhart & Co.
Edward Maitland
William Henry Making
Charles Martin
Mrs. Miller
Meyers Brothers
Morris & Co.
H. Moseley
Muggeridge & Co.
George Needham
New Civil Service Co-operation, Limited
Thomas Nixon
Stafford Northcote & Co.
Henry Herbert Oakley
Thomas O'Brien & Co.
Pawson & Co., Limited
Thomas Peacock
M. A. Phillips
H. G. Porter & Co.
William Porter, C.C.
Charles Price & Co.
Joseph Henry Price & Co.
Pilkington Bros.
Revellon Frères
Alexander Ritchie, C.C.
Adolphus Rosenthal
Rownson, Drew & Co.
Rev. William Russell
J. Russell & Co.
August de Grand Ry & Co.
Sargent & Co.
T. H. Saunders & Co.
T. & F. Schlund
John Shaw
Shugley & Flory
Benjamin Smith & Sons
Spence & Co.
Spiers & Pond, Limited
Stamp, Blatspiel & Co.
George Ratcliffe Steel
Steven Brothers & Co.
Storey & Triggs
Edmund Sumner
Stoer Brother & Coles' Office Staff
Tayler & Co.
Thomas & Sons
Thomson Brothers
George Thistle Thornes, C.C.
The Times Newspaper
Temperance Permanent Benefit Building Society
Todd & Proctor
Van der Beeck & Kuhler
Wilson, Salaman & Co.
J. W. Williams
R. Williams
The Window Cleaning Co.
Thomas Withey
E. Wolff & Co.
Worthington Engineering and Pumping Co.
Wright & Greig
Cyril Wyche

www.ingramcontent.com/pod-product-compliance
Lightning Source LLC
Chambersburg PA
CBHW020152170426
43199CB00010B/1006